Animal Groups

A Pod of Whales

by Lucia Raatma

PEBBLE
a capstone imprint

Pebble Plus is published by Pebble, a Capstone imprint, 1710 Roe Crest Drive,
North Mankato, Minnesota 56003 www.mycapstone.com

Library of Congress Cataloging-in-Publication Data
Names: Raatma, Lucia, author.
Title: A pod of whales / by Lucia Raatma.
Description: North Mankato, Minnesota : Pebble, [2020] | Series: Animal
    groups | Includes bibliographical references and index. | Audience: Age
    5-7. | Audience: K to Grade 3.
Identifiers: LCCN 2019003028 | ISBN 9781977109521 (library binding) | ISBN
    9781977110480 (paperback) | ISBN 9781977109583 (ebook pdf)
Subjects: LCSH: Whales—Behavior—Juvenile literature. | Social behavior in
    animals—Juvenile literature.
Classification: LCC QL737.C4 R18 2020 | DDC 599.5/45—dc23
LC record available at https://lccn.loc.gov/2019003028

Editorial Credits
Abby Colich, editor; Tracy McCabe, designer; Eric Gohl, media researcher;
Kathy McColley, production specialist

Photo Credits
Alamy: BIOSPHOTO, 15; Nature Picture Library: Tony Wu, 17; Newscom:
agefotostock/Michael S. Nolan, 11, George Karbus Photography Cultura, 9,
ZUMA Press/Media Drum World, 5; Science Source: Christopher Swann,
13; Shutterstock: katatonia82, cover (background), psirob, 21, Rich Carey,
background, Shirley W Images, back cover (bottom), 19, Tomas Kotouc, cover,
1, UWPhotog, back cover (top), 7

All internet sites appearing in back matter were available and accurate when
this book was sent to press.

Note to Parents and Teachers

The Animal Groups set supports national science standards
related to life science. This book describes and illustrates
life in a pod of whales. The images support early readers in
understanding the text. The repetition of words and phrases
helps early readers learn new words. This book also introduces
early readers to subject-specific vocabulary words, which
are defined in the Glossary section. Early readers may need
assistance to read some words and to use the Table of Contents,
Glossary, Read More, Internet Sites, Critical Thinking Questions,
and Index sections of the book.

Printed and bound in China.

1654

Table of Contents

What Is a Pod?

Splash! Huge whales jump out of the water. Whales live together in groups. A group of whales is called a pod. Pods live in all the oceans.

About three to 50 whales live in a pod. Some pods have up to 100 whales. One female leads the pod. Other females and their young live in the pod.

Swimming Together

A pod travels from place
to place. It swims to colder
waters. The pod looks for food.
It travels to warmer waters.
Here females give birth.

Females have one baby
at a time. The baby is called
a calf. Calves drink
their mother's milk. They stay
in the pod for several years.

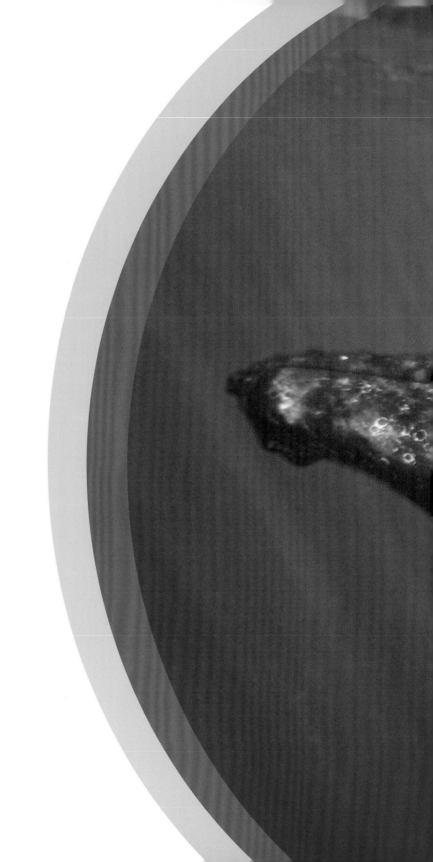

Young males leave the pod.

They look for mates.

Young females may explore
outside their pod.

But they usually return.

Time to Eat!

Whales look for food. Some whales eat plankton and other small sea life. The whales trap food with baleen. Baleen are like teeth.

baleen

Some whales eat large sea animals. The whales make sounds that bounce off objects. This helps whales find their prey. They swallow it whole.

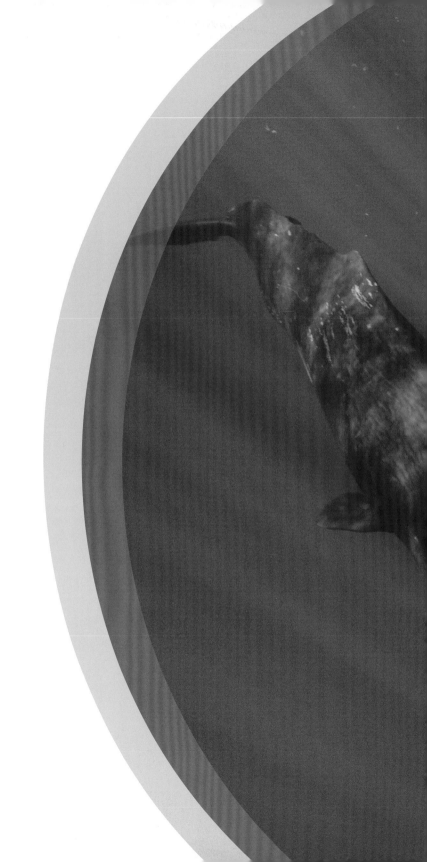

Whale Talk

Whales jump out of the water.
This is called breaching. The jump
can tell other whales to change
direction. Whales also breach
to see what is around them.

Whales sing too. They sing
to find mates. They also make
clicks and whistles.
Whales slap their tales.
This warns others of danger.

Glossary

baleen—long, fringed plates in the mouths of some whales

breach—to jump out of the water

calf—a young whale

mate—the male or female partner of a pair of animals that joins together to produce young

plankton—tiny plants and animals that drift in the ocean

prey—an animal hunted by another animal for food

Read More

Coleman, Clara. *Whales Work Together.* Animal Teamwork. New York: Powerkids Press, 2018.

Idzikowski, Lisa. *How Whales Grow Up.* Animals Growing Up. New York: Enslow, 2018.

Tunby, Benjamin. *The Whale's Journey.* Amazing Migrators. Minneapolis: Lerner, 2018.

Internet Sites

Enchanted Learning: All About Whales
https://www.enchantedlearning.com/subjects/whales/glossary/Pod.shtml

Science for Kids: Whale Facts
http://www.scienceforkidsclub.com/whale-facts.html

Whale Facts for Kids
https://www.whalefacts.org/whale-facts-for-kids/

Super-cool stuff! Check out projects, games, and lots more at www.capstonekids.com

Critical Thinking Questions

1. Why do pods travel?
2. What are the two different ways whales find food?
3. What is breaching? Why do whales breach?

Index